GREAT BRITISH COOKING

50 FAVOURITE RECIPES

(GE)

GREAT BRITISH COOKING

50 FAVOURITE RECIPES

JEREMY MILLS

Published by Great Editions

First Published 2021

Text and images © Jeremy Mills

The moral right of the author has been asserted.

All rights reserved. No part of this publication may be reproduced or transmitted in any form or by any means, electronic or mechanical, including photocopying, recording, or any information storage or retrieval system without prior permission in writing from the publishers.

Every effort has been made to trace copyright holders and to obtain their permission for the use of copyright material. The publisher apologises for any errors or omissions and would be grateful to be notified of any corrections that should be included in any future editions of this book.

Paperback ISBN: 978-1-911148-29-6

Hardback ISBN: 978-1-911148-30-2

EBook ISBN: 078-1-911148-31-9

CONTENTS

Foreword	i
About this book	iii – v

BREAKFASTS

Banana Bread	2
Fresh Muesli	3
Huevos Rancheros	4

STARTERS

Beef Carpaccio	6
Insalata Tricoloré	7
King Prawn Cocktail	8 – 9

LIGHT MAINS

Chicken Caesar Salad	12
Fusilli con Fagiolini e Pancetta	13
Macaroni and Cheese	14
Pizza Margherita	15
Penne al Arrabiata	16
Salade Niçoise	17
Salmone con Tagliatelle	18 – 19
Traffic Light Pasta Salad	20

MAINS

Aloo Keema Curry	22 – 23
Baked Rainbow Trout	24
Beef Olives with Black Pudding	25
Beef Stroganoff	26
Beef Tacos	27
Bobotie	28 – 29
Butter Chicken Delhi Style	30 – 31
Chicken Dopiaza	32 – 33
Chicken Karahi	34 – 35
Chicken Provençal	36
Chicken Schenkel	37
Chicken Tikka Masala	38 – 39
Chilli con Carne	40 – 41
Cod with Chorizo and Beans	42 – 43
Curried Shepherd's Pie	44 – 45
Keema Curry with Potatoes and Green Beans	46 – 47
Keralan Malabar Prawns	48 – 49
Lamb Rogan Josh	50 – 51
Meatball Black Bean Chilli	52 – 53
Moussaka	54
Mutton Koftas	55
Ossobucco	56
Pollo Fajitas	57
Pork Steak with Creamy Blue Cheese Relish	58
Paella	59
Spaghetti Bolognese	60 – 61
Striploin Steak with Hot Tomato Sauce	62 – 63
Sweet and Sour Chicken	64 – 65
Sage Stuffed Chicken Breasts	66
Tandoori Chicken with Roasted Sweet Potatoes	67
Thirteen Minute Corn	68 – 69
Trevigiana Spaghetti	70

DESSERTS

Pear Tarte Tatin	72 – 73
Raspberry Soufflé	74 – 75
Tiramisú	76

YOUR RECIPES

DEDICATION

for Adriane
with love and
heartfelt thanks
for everything

FOREWORD

This book features some of Britain's favourite dishes of the last 50 years. It also contains my own favourite recipes. Then finally, there is space in the book for you to insert your own favourite recipe to personalise this copy for yourself or as a gift to family or friends. Once you have added your recipe *Great British Cooking – 50 Favourite Recipes* will be complete and unique.

Why did I write this book? First and foremost, I am a book designer, editor, publisher and printer. I have worked in book publishing, design, colour printing and bookbinding in various capacities. Over the years, I also developed my ideas about cooking, so researching this book has been a long term journey.

I started printing as an activity at school and then bought my own equipment which I installed in the cellar of my mother's two bed semi in Ipswich and I soon built up a good customer base. I was considering continuing my career as a jobbing printer in the cellar of my Mother's house, when an opportunity arose to become a trainee manager at a reputable Suffolk book printer, Cowells of Ipswich.

The Company was founded in 1818 and had a rich history of high quality typography and book design. The books were printed on large sheet fed presses and bound on an automated book line. They included titles on cooking, gardening and walking. It was too good an opportunity to turn down. I could always run my own business later with a bit more experience under my belt.

Some years later, after attending college and working for Cowells as a management trainee I left to study for an MBA (Masters of Business Administration) at Durham University Business School. I went on to work in business and management positions before starting my own publishing business in 2003.

A few years after starting my business, I began to compile a list of my favourite recipes, with the aim of writing and publishing a cookery book. Over time, I cooked or prepared each recipe, made notes, adjusted or experimented and then edited and re-wrote the recipes as necessary.

My aim was to present 50 recipes which rather than actually being traditional British cooking, reflected life in Britain and the diverse cultures that have influenced our cuisine in the last 50 or so years. Some of the recipes, of course, have stood the test of time better than others, and these I have updated and modernised. They comprise the majority of this book.

The remainder of the recipes are my personal favourites. Hopefully, you will add yours too at the end of the book to complete the title: *Great British Cooking – 50 Favourite Recipes*

Jeremy Mills, Huddersfield, January 2021.

ABOUT THIS BOOK

To help you navigate your way through this book, here is an explanation and information about the preparation, cooking and presentation of the recipes.

FRESH SEASONAL INGREDIENTS

In the last 50 years it has become increasingly commonplace to be able to buy different types of fruit, vegetables and other products from around the world in British supermarkets at any time of the year. As a result, many people are no longer as focussed on freshness and seasonality as they once were. Food manufacturers and supermarkets often sell unripe fruit and vegetables in order to gain a longer shelf life and less food wastage.

I would prefer to buy fully ripened tomatoes, freshly picked strawberries, newly podded peas or freshly dug potatoes and all organic please with no single use plastic (see page v)! I encourage you to cook dishes where the key ingredients are fresh, ripe and organically grown. Make the most of the good, fresh seasonal produce. It also saves on your grocery bills!

GROW YOUR OWN

Please grow your own vegetables and fruit whenever you can, even if you have limited space, but only use organic methods. A few pots with herbs on a window ledge or a grow bag with potatoes on a balcony, anything is better than nothing. Growing your own vegetables and fruit is a pleasing and relaxing activity that helps your mind and saves money.

READY MEALS AND PRE-PREPARED FOOD

In Britain we have moved away from cooking dishes from inception with fresh ingredients, instead buying ready meals, takeaways and other pre-prepared items. While this saves some time and effort it can be quite expensive and the prepared products may contain some pretty unsavoury ingredients, excessive sugars and chemical additives which you wouldn't dream of adding to your cooking if you were preparing the meal yourself!

The advent of widespread ownership of fridges and freezers in the 1960s allowed consumers to buy a much wider range of these products and store them for longer, further discouraging real home cooking.

The food manufacturers and supermarkets have advertised and encouraged us to buy pre-prepared meals and this has meant that many people no longer cook using fresh ingredients and have lost basic cooking skills. Unfortunately, there are too many 'Buy One, Get One Free' offers, too many 'meal deals' and too many pre-prepared items.

NUTRITION, PORTION SIZES AND FOOD WASTE

In the recipes in this book I use mainly fresh ingredients and I avoid using ingredients like full fat butter, cream and sugar whenever possible.

This is not a diet book and I am not a nutritionist, so I have not measured the exact calorific or fat content of each recipe, but most are fairly healthy if consumed in reasonable-sized portions. The estimate of portion size is based on a fully grown adult with an average body weight who indulges in some form of exercise a couple of times each week and wishes to maintain approximately the same weight. The reality is that people of different ages, body types and sizes and activity/exercise levels require different quantities of food, so I am leaving the matter of portion size to the reader's choice.

In most cases, I try to serve a portion size that will be eaten without the person leaving any on the plate which will need to be thrown away. Throwing away food you have made or buying too much and then having to throw it out is very bad and wasteful on pretty much every level.

Planning meals (like the recipes in this book) is a very good way of reducing waste and buying exact quantities of the necessary ingredients certainly helps the fight against food waste.

Much better to serve the right amount of a good recipe and put any leftovers in the fridge for lunch the next day.

PREPARATION AND COOKING TIMES

Not many of us want to spend hours on end preparing gourmet meals every day, so I have tried to ensure that nearly all the recipes in this book are well within the reach of most families, both in terms of complexity and cost. Many can be prepared in advance or in larger quantities for freezing and some are cooked with a slow cooker for convenience, flavour and flexibility.

Oven temperatures listed are for a fan-assisted oven, if yours is not, then please add 20°C to the cooking temperatures. I would recommend using a separate oven thermometer and a meat one so that you can check oven temperatures and whether things are properly cooked.

SPICES AND FLAVOURINGS

At home, we maintain a fairly well-stocked spice rack, containing about 60 different spices and flavourings which are kept in a dark, cool stone larder (which was built at the same time as our house in 1958, before the days of widespread modern refrigeration). It has thick stone shelves and is good for storing many different types of produce.

Most spices lose their flavour if kept too long or if stored in bright or warm conditions, so a larder cupboard is ideal as the temperature is relatively constant, if not any cool store cupboard would suffice.

Pepper and salt are not listed in the ingredient lists for recipes as I am also assuming that you have access to a good salt and pepper grinder and have fresh peppercorns and good quality coarse sea salt, if not please go out and buy them!

KITCHEN EQUIPMENT

Ideally, you should have a double oven and grill, a gas hob, a good-sized, high quality fridge/freezer and a slow cooker. Many of the recipes use the slow cooker. I also recommend a tiered, lidded steamer for vegetables.

Other useful things to have include a stick blender, a good quality grater with grating options (fine, medium etc), a good set of kitchen knives and a knife sharpener.

PLASTIC PACKAGING

In recent years, there finally seems to be some international impetus to ban single use plastic. Hopefully, this will happen sooner rather than later. The majority of single use plastic packaging should probably be banned with immediate effect. Meats, cheese, vegetables and fruit do not need to be supplied in plastic trays and plastic drinks containers should go the same way.

A good way to avoid this supermarket-style packaging is to shop at farmers' markets or fresh produce counters. Although it can be hard work finding everything you need, it is certainly worth making an effort.

COMPOSTING

It is a good idea to have a small, lidded composting bin in the kitchen which can be used for most raw vegetable peelings, tea bags, coffee grounds and paper/card waste. Some items don't compost or break down very well such as egg shells, avocado skins and pits, but cardboard egg boxes and toilet roll paperboard cores are useful additions and break down easily.

I regularly empty our composting caddy into the main compost bin in the corner of the garden. I turn the compost every now and then and then replace the lid to keep in the moisture and heat and then let the composting bugs do their work. Once the compost is ready, I use it to mulch the vegetable beds and hopefully grow better crops.

AND FINALLY

I hope you have found this section helpful and good luck with the cooking, I hope you find it fun, healthy, relaxing and economical.

BREAKFASTS

BANANA BREAD

I am a bit of a Yorkshire cheapskate, something that is probably a mixture of nature and nurture, having a Bradford-born Mother, who spent a lot of time scraping around in the bottom of jam jars and lecturing about food waste. This has been followed by me spending a lengthy spell living in the North of England. A couple of years ago, I was faced with the domestic problem of having to deal with two bananas that were overripe and looked like they were destined for the compost heap. That was when I discovered this recipe, an antidote to the awful wastage of overripe bananas.

RECIPE

Serves 4
Preparation Time – 20 minutes
Cooking Time – 45 minutes

INGREDIENTS

150g caster sugar
150g salted butter at room temperature
2 large eggs, beaten
150g self-raising flour
1 tsp baking powder
2 very ripe bananas, mashed

METHOD

Heat the oven to 180°C and butter a 900g loaf tin and line with baking parchment.

Mix the sugar and butter together until well combined then slowly add the eggs with a little of the flour, a little at a time, blending all the time.

Now fold in the remaining flour, mashed banana and baking powder, making sure it is all well distributed.

Pour into the baking tin and bake in the oven for 35 minutes.

Leave to cool for 10 minutes, then remove to a wire rack and either cut into slices and serve straightway or store in an airtight container once fully cooled.

FRESH MUESLI

This recipe was passed on to me by my friends in Ipswich, Andrew and Lynn Young, and now I am going to share it with you.

This is a very quick, healthy and easy way to start the day. I don't always eat breakfast so this is an ideal mid-morning snack for when you are busy working, which I usually am!

RECIPE

Serves 4
Preparation Time – 5 minutes

INGREDIENTS

300g plain, low fat yoghurt
8 tbsp plain oats
2 tbsp raisins
2 coarsely grated dessert apples with skins left on
2 lemons zest and juice
4 tbsp local, organic runny honey
2 tbsp chopped hazelnuts

METHOD

Grate the lemons into a bowl and add the lemon juice.

Then grate the apples coarsely and add them to the bowl, coating with the lemon juice and rind to prevent them going brown.

Now fold in the yoghurt, raisins and oats.

Serve in bowls with honey spooned on top and sprinkled with the chopped hazelnuts.

HUEVOS RANCHEROS

Huevos rancheros or rancher's eggs is a Mexican vegetarian breakfast dish with a spicy kick like a burro! The tomatoes should be absolutely fresh, big and juicy, not green and hard! This is easy to make with largely store cupboard ingredients and makes an excellent brunch.

RECIPE

Serves 4
Preparation Time – 20 minutes
Cooking Time – 20 minutes

INGREDIENTS

Pico de Gallo
2 large, fully ripe tomatoes, chopped
1 large onion, finely chopped
50g fresh coriander, chopped
1 lime, zest and juice

Beans
1 x 400g tin black beans
1 onion, finely chopped
2 garlic cloves, finely chopped
2 tbsp olive oil
1 tsp ground cumin

The Rest
4 large eggs
4 corn tortillas
200g Monterey Jack (or similar such as Gouda or Edam), coarsely grated
1 ripe avocado, stoned and skin removed, roughly chopped
Tabasco or chilli sauce to serve

METHOD

Prepare the Pico de Gallo in a medium bowl by combining the ingredients, seasoning and then set to one side, retaining a tablespoon or so of lime juice for the bean mixture.

To make the bean mixture, start by gently sautéeing the onions and garlic in the olive oil for approx. 5 minutes. Add the ground cumin and then the drained can of beans and 100 ml or so of water together with some seasoning.

Cover and cook on medium heat for 5 minutes stirring occasionally, then roughly mash the mixture and carry on cooking uncovered for a further 3 or 4 minutes. Remove from the heat, add the remaining lime juice, cover and keep warm.

Warm the tortillas on both sides one at a time in a skillet, remove and keep warm and then gently fry the eggs in the same pan with a little olive oil until cooked through.

To serve, place a tortilla each on four plates. Spoon and spread out the bean mix on each tortilla and cover with the shredded cheese. Lift the eggs from the pan and place one in the centre of each tortilla. Spoon the Pico de Gallo on top and add the avocado pieces and sauce with a little more coriander and black pepper if desired.

STARTERS

BEEF CARPACCIO

This is a delicious starter which is very much reliant on really high quality beef with all fat removed. This recipe calls for 4-5 days marinading time so is an ideal dinner party dish or meal for entertaining (provided you remember to start preparing well in advance!). This dish was named after the Italian painter, Vittore Carpaccio who was known for the red and white colours in his work. The dish is made from raw beef, olive oil and grated Parmesan cheese.

RECIPE

Serves 4
Preparation Time – 30 minutes
Marinading Time – 4-5 days

WINE PAIRING

Cabernet Sauvignon

INGREDIENTS

750g Aberdeen Angus beef topside, all fat and sinew removed

Marinade

600ml olive oil
400ml balsamic vinegar
300ml dry white wine
3 tbsp dark soy sauce
3 tbsp Worcestershire sauce
1 bunch of fresh basil, roughly chopped
1 small bunch of thyme
20 crushed black peppercorns
15g coarse sea salt

To serve

Parmesan cheese, sliced into shavings

METHOD

Mix together all the marinade ingredients into a large non-metallic bowl, keeping back some basil leaves for serving.

The beef should be rolled in the marinade and left to steep in the fridge for 4-5 days to achieve the desired taste. The beef should be turned every day to ensure consistency throughout.

The meat is removed at the end of the marinading process and firmly wrapped in cling film. It can now be frozen and sliced thinly from frozen as required or sliced thinly from the fridge ready for serving with the marinade.

Before serving the marinade over the thin, raw beef slices it is necessary to push it through a sieve. Parmesan shavings and torn basil leaves can be scattered over the top and finished with a few twists of fresh black pepper.

INSALATA TRICOLORÉ

I think this is my favourite Italian starter and it uses the red, white and green colours of the Italian flag, very clever! I wonder what we could make out of the Union Jack? It is essential that all the ingredients are fresh and fully ripe, no green supermarket tomatoes please and make sure those avocados are just ripe! The other easy Italian salads you can try are *insalata caprese* and *insalata bocconcini* if you like this recipe.

RECIPE

Serves 4
Preparation Time – 15 minutes

WINE PAIRING

Light Italian rosé or sparkling rosé.

INGREDIENTS

4 ripe tomatoes
2 ripe avocados, pitted and sliced
200g fresh mozzarella
2 tbsp olive oil
2 tbsp balsamic vinegar
Small bunch fresh basil

METHOD

Halve and slice the tomatoes into large bite size pieces and arrange them on a large serving plate.

Place an avocado slice and a slice of mozzarella on top of each and drizzle the olive oil and balsamic vinegar on top. Tear the basil leaves and scatter over.

Season with freshly ground pepper and salt if desired.

KING PRAWN COCKTAIL

The ubiquitous 1970s Prawn Cocktail wasn't a dish that I had a great deal of time for really, rather naff in its Englishness and bland with its iceberg lettuce and small grub-like prawns. However, a trip to Nerja in Spain in 2019 was a revelation. We sat at an outside table in an upmarket seafood restaurant in glorious late Spring sunshine and the people at the adjacent table were served prawn cocktails. These were prawn cocktails re-imagined, not little cheap wine glasses but big wine bowl glasses, with a bed of fresh green salad leaves, steeped with fresh avocado and firm, large and juicy king prawns with a rich pink sauce, topped off with fresh, bright paprika and big succulent lemon wedges cut over the edge of the glasses. I ordered one for myself obviously! Here is the recipe, but make sure you buy really good king prawns, mega-fresh leafy lettuce and top quality lemons, the freshness is critical!

RECIPE

Serves 4
Preparation Time – 10 minutes

WINE PAIRING

This is definitely a Summer/hot weather dish, so something cold and sparkling like Cava or Prosecco

INGREDIENTS

20-24 large, cooked king prawns, head and shell removed (or cook the raw ones if you prefer)
Romaine, or gem and round lettuce, shredded
2 fully ripe avocados, pitted and cut into slices

Rose Marie Sauce
1 tbsp tomato ketchup
4 tbsp mayonnaise
1 tsp lemon juice and one lemon cut into wedges
1 tsp Worcester sauce
Salt and pepper to season
1 tsp paprika

METHOD

Make the Rose Marie sauce by combining the ketchup, mayonnaise, Worcester sauce and lemon juice with a seasoning of salt and pepper.

Take 4 large wine glasses and arrange the salad leaves at the base and either layer the avocado on top or against the side of the glasses.

Drop the king prawns onto the bed of lettuce and spoon the sauce over the prawns (carefully). Sprinkle over the paprika and clip the lemon wedges over the rims of the glasses (and add a king prawn to the rims if you like). Serve straightaway, this recipe must be as fresh as possible!

LIGHT MAINS

CHICKEN CAESAR SALAD

This dish was invented by Caesar Cardini, an Italian restaurateur at his restaurant in San Diego in 1924. He also ran a restaurant across the border at Tijuana, thereby circumventing the restrictions of Prohibition at the time. The salad grew to be a global culinary sensation in the coming years and in the 1940s, Gourmet Magazine called the dish 'the gastronomic highlight of the current moment'. This version below was first made by me in 2006, and quite regularly since.

RECIPE

Serves 4
Preparation Time – 20 minutes
Cooking Time – 20 minutes

WINE PAIRING

Prosecco or other light sparkling wine, but don't rule out a red like Malbec

INGREDIENTS

4 boneless, skinless chicken breasts
2 tbsp olive oil
2 Romaine lettuces, washed and chopped roughly
4 thick slices of baguette
16 cherry tomatoes, halved (optional)

Dressing
1 tbsp fish sauce or 4 anchovy fillets chopped
6 tbsp mayonnaise
1 tbsp lemon juice
1 tbsp olive oil
1 tsp Worcester Sauce
1 tsp Dijon mustard
3 garlic cloves crushed
50g Parmigiano-Reggiano, finely grated

METHOD

Prepare the chicken breasts by taking each one and placing between 2 sheets of cling film or greaseproof paper and beat with a rolling pin until about 1 cm thick.

Mix all the dressing ingredients together in a small bowl and leave in the fridge covered.

Arrange the lettuce in a large, non-metallic serving bowl and add the tomatoes on top if desired. Toast the baguette slices in the griddle pan in olive oil and lightly brown both sides. Remove from the pan and cut the slices into pieces of approx. 2 cm and add to the serving bowl scattered on top.

Oil the griddle pan and place the chicken breasts two 2 at a time in the pan (depending on the size of the pan), season and sauté both sides for approx. 3 minutes each on a medium heat until partly browned and cooked through. Set aside and keep warm. Now, slice the warm chicken into bite sized strips and scatter into the serving bowl.

Finally, either lightly stir in the dressing or place the dressing bowl on the dining table with the chicken salad bowl and serving spoons for people to help themselves with more Parmesan and black pepper to grind on top.

FUSILLI CON FAGIOLINI E PANCETTA

Obviously, what and how you cook and your recipes are guided by many things including your background, family and friends, how much money you have and where you live and what ingredients are available. This recipe originally came from Ontario, Canada where some of my family members live and where I have sent most summers for the last 25 years or so.

I was up at the cottage on Lake Huron where shopping for provisions involves a 7 mile boat ride to the nearest dock and then a drive to the nearest store. So, cooking is often quite simple and relies on what is actually in the cottage (unless when out fishing you catch a bass, salmon or pike). One day, I was flicking through a cookery magazine and I saw this recipe because it was a light summer dish and also because I just happened to have all the ingredients available to me, although I substituted the pancetta here with smoked bacon. The beans I used were fresh Ontario beans and locally grown onions both of which are often sold at roadside stalls in the summer in Canada and the parsley was growing in a pot by the entrance to the cottage. I hope you like it.

RECIPE

Serves 4
Preparation Time – 10 minutes
Cooking time – 15 minutes

WINE PAIRING

Prosecco or a Pinot Noir

INGREDIENTS

300g fusilli or other twisted pasta
8 rashers of smoked bacon or pancetta
200g fresh green beans, trimmed and chopped
1 tbsp olive oil
1 bunch spring onions
200g mushrooms, sliced
4 tbsp crème fraîche or similar
2 tbsp chopped parsley

METHOD

Cook the pasta in boiling, salted water according to the pack instructions until it is *al dente*, normally around 12 minutes for dried fusilli and then drain and set aside, covered.

Once the pasta is on, grill the bacon until almost crisp, then chop into pieces approx. 3 cm long.

Blanche the green beans in a pan of boiling, salted water for approx. 2 minutes and then immediately drain and rinse them in very cold water, to keep them crisp and brightly coloured.

Heat the oil in a large pan and gently fry the onions and mushrooms for around 4 minutes.

Add the beans, bacon and crème fraîche and gently heat through.

Serve the bacon and bean sauce over a bed of fusilli and garnish with the parsley sprinkled over.

MACARONI AND CHEESE

The cheese sauce is added to the macaroni and baked just long enough to turn golden on the top. For a good, crisp topping, sprinkle buttered breadcrumbs on top before baking. Made freshly, it tastes so much better than the packet variety.

RECIPE

Serves 4
Preparation Time – 15 minutes
Cooking Time – 20 minutes

INGREDIENTS

400g fresh macaroni
3 tbsp butter
2 tbsp plain flour
Pinch of onion powder or onion salt
Pinch of garlic powder
1 tbsp Dijon mustard
1 tbsp Worcester sauce
300 ml milk
250g cheddar cheese, grated
200 ml fresh breadcrumbs

METHOD

Pre heat the oven to 190°C.

Bring a pan of salted water to the boil and cook the macaroni quickly cook the macaroni according to instructions.

Meanwhile, melt half the butter in a large saucepan over medium heat. Stir in the flour and seasonings with salt and pepper if desired.

Gradually add the milk, a little at a time stirring constantly until the mixture thickens.

Add the cheese reserving some for the topping. Remove from the heat and added the drained macaroni and stir to combine.

Pour into a pre-greased casserole dish, sprinkle with the reserved cheese.

Melt the remaining butter and fry the breadcrumbs for a few minutes until crisp. Scatter on top of the macaroni and bake in the oven for 15 minutes.

PIZZA MARGHERITA

This popular main course is another Italian dish, which like the *insalata tricolore* recipe, displays the colours of the Italian flag and was concocted by Pizza-maker Raffaele Esposito in Naples in 1889 as a homage to Queen Margherita de Saboya; it's not every day you get a pizza named after you!

The secret with pizzas is to use a wood-fired pizza oven, failing that an oven that operates at a very high temperature, ideally around 280°C of higher or you can use a pizza stone around 240°C which retains a lot of heat and helps to crisp up the base of the pizza. The high temperature ensures that the crust is crisp, the cheese nicely melted and the cooking time is quick to reduce the chances of the pizza drying out.

RECIPE

Serves 4
Preparation Time – 2 hours 30 minutes (for the dough)
Cooking time – 15-20 minutes

WINE PAIRING

Light Italian rosé

INGREDIENTS

The Dough
500g plain flour
30g fresh yeast
125ml water
2 tbsp olive oil

Topping
4 large ripe tomatoes, peeled, deseeded and chopped
450g fresh mozzarella, diced
2 tbsp olive oil

To Serve
Small bunch fresh basil, torn

METHOD

To make the dough, firstly dissolve the yeast in a little warm water in a large bowl. Add two or three tablespoons of flour and stir with a wooden spoon until an even mass has formed. Cover with a cloth and leave to rest for 30 minutes.

Sift the remaining flour onto a work surface and mix with the first dough mixture. Divide the dough into four balls, sprinkle a little flour over and leave to rest, covered for 2 hours.

Heat the oven to 240 - 280°C.

Now, roll out each ball to make a thin circular pizza base. Arrange the tomatoes and mozzarella slices evenly over each base and drizzle some olive oil on top and season.

Bake, ideally on a pizza stone, for 15 minutes.

Remove from oven, cut with a pizza cutter, sprinkle over the basil and a little extra olive oil and serve straight away.

PENNE AL ARRABIATA

Tasty and quick, pasta quills with chilli sauce is a simple dish, but one which is highly dependent on the quality and freshness of the tomatoes and pasta.

RECIPE

Serves 4
Preparation Time – 15 minutes
Cooking Time – 20 minutes

WINE PAIRING

Crisp white such as Pinot Grigio or Gavi

INGREDIENTS

400g fresh tomatoes, skinned, deseeded and chopped
2 tbsp olive oil
2 garlic cloves, crushed
2 red chilli peppers, deseeded and finely chopped
2 tbsp tomato purée
1 tsp caster sugar
350g fresh penne (pasta quills)
2 tbsp parsley, chopped

METHOD

Prepare the tomatoes by plunging them into a pan of boiling water to loosen the skins. Remove the skins, hard tops and seeds. Chop finely and set aside.

Heat the olive oil in a large pan and gently fry the onion, garlic and chilli peppers for a few minutes. Add the tomatoes, sugar and tomato purée and continue cooking gently for 15 minutes, stirring regularly.

Meanwhile, cook the pasta so that it is *al dente* and ready at the same time as the sauce.

Drain the pasta and add the sauce to the pasta with the parsley and toss thoroughly prior to serving. Season with salt and pepper as desired.

SALADE NIÇOISE

One of the best salads around and great for a summer light lunch, in fact I could eat one right now!

RECIPE

Serves 4
Preparation Time – 20 minutes
Cooking Time – 15 minutes

WINE PAIRING

Light rosé

INGREDIENTS

4 eggs
250g tinned tuna fish
4 ripe vine tomatoes
16 black olives, pitted
1 Romaine lettuce
8 anchovy fillets

VINAIGRETTE DRESSING

4 tbsp olive oil
2 tbsp red wine vinegar
1 tbsp Dijon mustard
1 garlic clove, crushed
400ml balsamic vinegar

METHOD

Hard boil the eggs, cool them under cold running water, shell them and carefully slice the eggs in half. Drain and flake the tuna.

Mix together all the vinaigrette ingredients in a large non-metallic bowl. Toss in and coat the lettuce leaves.

Arrange the eggs, tomatoes cut into wedges with the black olives and strips of anchovy on top of the lettuce and pile the flaked tuna in the centre. Serve with salad servers.

SALMONE CON TAGLIATELLE

When I first started work after leaving college I soon bought my first house, a two bed terrace on Withipoll Street in Ipswich for £15,800. Funny name, and a funny street really, it was named after Sir Edmund Withipoll who founded nearby Christchurch Park. My lodgers included Guy Robson, nephew of the then England football manager, Bobby Robson and Bernhard who watched the whole of Band Aid on the front room TV in 1984. This recipe was one of my more sophisticated dishes from that time.

RECIPE

Serves 4
Preparation Time – 5 minutes
Cooking Time – 10 minutes

WINE PAIRING

Sauvignon Blanc

INGREDIENTS

500g atlantic or pacific salmon, poached
6 tbsp olive oil
1 lemon, finely grated zest and juice
3 cloves of garlic, finely chopped
500g fresh tagliatelle
1 handful of fresh parsley chopped

METHOD

Break the poached salmon flesh into large flakes.

Heat a large pan of salted water and once boiling, cook the tagliatelle for 3 minutes.

Meanwhile, put the salmon flakes in a large saucepan and toss lightly with the oil, lemon juice and zest, garlic and season as desired.

Gently warm over a low heat.

Drain the pasta well, and add to the large saucepan, tossing lightly with the other ingredients and garnish with the parsley when serving. Serve immediatemente!

TRAFFIC LIGHT PASTA SALAD

This is a very simple recipe which I learnt while a printing student at college in Watford. It is ideal for a snack, a packed lunch or mixed with cold meats, flaked tuna, cooked prawns or cheese. It keeps very well in the fridge in a container and it has been a regular feature in our household since those Watford days.

RECIPE

Serves 4
Preparation – 5 minutes
Cooking Time – 10 minutes

WINE PAIRING

Maybe a light red

INGREDIENTS

400g fresh pasta shells (Conchiglie)
1 red bell pepper, deseeded ad chopped into 1 cm pieces
250g tinned sweetcorn
250g frozen or fresh peas
1 tbsp olive oil

METHOD

Cook pasta according to instructions, drain, rinse in cold water and allow to cool.

Cook the peas and sweetcorn in salted boiling water, drain and rinse in cold water.

Tip all the vegetables and pasta into a large bowl or lidded container, add the oil, season and stir.

This can now be served straight away or kept in the fridge.

MAINS

ALOO KEEMA CURRY

In 2009 my wife and I went to a comedy and curry cooking night in Holmfirth to see Glaswegian Punjabi chef Hardeep Singh Kohli and a very good show it was too. Hardeep cooked his keema curry for the audience and although I can't recall his exact recipe, it did lead me to start experimenting with my own version of a mince and potato curry suitable for the whole family.

RECIPE

Serves 4
Preparation Time – 20 minutes
Cooking Time – 30 minutes

WINE PAIRING

Chardonnay unoaked or a light red such as Beaujolais

INGREDIENTS

2 tbsp vegetable oil
1 onion, chopped
1 tbsp grated, fresh root ginger
3 garlic cloves, crushed
2 tbsp medium curry powder
1 tbsp chilli powder
500g minced beef
2 tbsp tomato purée
250 ml beef stock
750g new potatoes
200g frozen peas
6 tbsp plain yoghurt
Fresh mint leaves, torn

METHOD

In a heavy pan fry the onions, ginger and garlic in the oil over medium heat for approx. 5 minutes until lightly browned at the edges, stirring constantly. Set aside in a separate bowl to cool slightly. Whizz this mixture with a stick blender with a little water until it becomes a smooth paste.

Add the new potatoes to a saucepan of cold water and bring to the boil and simmer for approx. 10 minutes.

Using the same heavy pan add the minced beef brown it. Add the spices, cooked potatoes, beef stock, seasoning and tomato purée and simmer for 5 minutes.

Finally, add the peas and continue cooking until the peas are cooked through, approximately 5 minutes.

Serve the curry with rice or naan bread accompanied by raita of yoghurt and mint leaves.

BAKED RAINBOW TROUT

A really tasty, economical supper, particularly if you have caught the trout yourself, which I have on more than one occasion.

RECIPE

Serves 4
Preparation Time – 10 minutes
Cooking Time – 20 minutes

WINE PAIRING

New Zealand Sauvignon Blanc

INGREDIENTS

4 Rainbow trout, gutted (so would you be if you had just been caught!)
3 tbsp plain flour
3 tbsp butter
150g small button mushrooms, sliced
1 tbsp lemon juice
3 medium onions, chopped
6 tbsp breadcrumbs (2 slices soft bread)

METHOD

Preheat the oven to 200°C.

Clean fish in cold water, pat dry, season and roll in the flour.

Melt 2 tablespoons of the butter in a large frying pan on medium heat. When the foam subsides add the trout and cook for approx. 5 minutes each side until golden.

Meanwhile, melt half the remaining butter in another frying pan over medium heat. Add the mushrooms and lemon juice and sauté for 2 minutes, stirring regularly. Remove from the pan and line a greased baking dish with the mushrooms.

Melt the remaining butter in the same pan and cook the onions for a further 2 minutes. Remove and set aside.

Now add the breadcrumbs to the same pan and cook in the remaining juices, stirring all the time until the breadcrumbs are golden (about 3 minutes).

Arrange the trout on top of the mushrooms in the baking dish, sprinkle with onions and buttered breadcrumbs and bake in the oven, uncovered for 10 minutes.

BEEF OLIVES WITH BLACK PUDDING

This recipe is an ideal dinner party dish or meal for entertaining as it is mostly prepared in advance and is slow cooked for two hours allowing plenty of time for talking and drinks.

RECIPE

Serves 4
Preparation Time – 30 minutes
Cooking Time – 2 hours

WINE PAIRING

Cabernet Sauvignon

INGREDIENTS

750g Aberdeen Angus beef, thinly sliced
200g minced chicken or turkey
3 medium onions, finely chopped
3 garlic cloves, finely chopped
6 sage leaves, chopped
1 tsp fresh thyme, chopped
200g black pudding, minced
200g button mushrooms, minced and cooked until dried out
1.5l gravy made with 250ml red wine
2 beef stock cubes
1 egg
1 tbsp vegetable oil

Garnish
100g button mushrooms
100g button onions
100g bacon, diced
100g butter
Chopped parsley

METHOD

Turn on the slow cooker to medium and pour in the red wine and water and add the crumbled stock cubes.

To make the filling mix the black pudding with the chicken mince, season and add the egg.

Sauté the onion, garlic and herbs in a little oil until softened and allow to cool.

Mix in the meat mixture and add the mushrooms.

Cut the beef into 8 slices and sit each slice between two sheets of cling film. Flatten with a rolling pin or mallet. Remove the cling film and spoon the filling into the centre of each slice of beef. Fold in the rough edges and roll each into a cylindrical shape. Pierce and hold in place with cocktail sticks.

Now fry the beef olives in butter or oil in a large frying pan until well coloured all over and add to the red wine gravy in the slow cooker. Cook on medium for approx. 2 hours, checking periodically, skimming off any fat or impurities.

Shortly before serving, start to prepare the garnish by frying the onions until golden. Remove from the pan and add the mushrooms and bacon until browned.

Serve two beef olives to each diner, garnished with the bacon, mushrooms and onions with parsley sprinkled over.

BEEF STROGANOFF

This dish was a popular dinner party dish in the 60s and I think I first attempted it in the 1980s. It has fallen out of popularity now but is actually OK, particularly if you like mushrooms and this version is certainly fairly mushroom-centric! Originally prepared by French chefs, it became popular in Russia and then moved onto the USA and Europe post World War II. It is very easy to prepare, but it needs a long time in the slow cooker to ensure that the beef strips are tenderised, so probably best prepared in the morning and then served early evening, quite handy if you have to work during the day and come home tired and are not much interested in cooking a meal. It is not necessary, but probably works best to brown up the beef in a heavy pan at the outset and also seal the onions and the mushrooms in the wok prior to transferring to the slow cooker.

RECIPE

Serves 4
Preparation Time – 30 minutes
Cooking Time – about 8 hours in the slow cooker

WINE PAIRING

A rich fruity red such as Shiraz or Grenache, alternatively a dry rosé would work well.

INGREDIENTS

500g beef steak, cut into bite sized strips
400g tin of condensed cream of chicken soup
200ml beef stock
3 tbsp Henderson's relish
3 cloves of garlic, crushed
1 tsp freshly ground black pepper
2 medium onions, coarsely chopped
200g small white button mushrooms
120ml soured cream
300g fresh tagliatelle
2 tbsp parsley, chopped, to garnish

METHOD

Brown up the beef strips in a wok with a little oil over medium heat and set aside. Seal the onions and then the mushrooms in the same wok.

Put all but the final soured cream, tagliatelle and parsley in the slow cooker and stir gently. Then leave to cook through slowly for approx. 8 hours.

When you think it is almost done, add the soured cream and season to taste. Cook for another 15 minutes or so and then serve on a bed of tagliatelle with parsley sprinkled on top.

BEEF TACOS

Although it had been around for a long time, Mexican food really took off in Britain in the 2010s and the number of restaurants and chains serving it grew considerably, some good, some bad. Popular dishes include burritos, tortillas, quesadillas and tacos. Tacos are a Mexican street food and they make for a pretty messy meal with crispy corn shells and lots of fillings, but it is a good meal that everyone can get involved with, choosing what and how much they want in each taco shell. This one is made with minced beef and spices (not a packet mix!) and is served with a variety of toppings of choice (see below). Please don't buy the pre-made shop guacamole which is unpleasant and full of preservatives, it needs to be made very fresh, and the same goes for the tomato salsa if you want that as well.

RECIPE

Serves 4
Preparation Time – 20 minutes
Cooking Time – 20 minutes

WINE PAIRING

Probably best to have a Corona beer with a lime wedge

INGREDIENTS

Beef mixture
500g lean minced beef
1 tbsp ground cumin
1 tbsp medium chili powder
1 tsp oregano, dried
2 tbsp tomato purée
Salt and pepper to season
12 x Taco shells

Optional Toppings
Cheddar cheese, coarsely grated
Shredded lettuce
Soured cream
Tomatoes, chopped (or tomato salsa)
Avocado, chopped (or guacamole)
Jalapeños, chopped

METHOD

Preheat the oven to about 100°C.

Add the minced beef to a large, heavy based pan with a little vegetable oil and cook over a medium heat, breaking up the minced beef and stirring continuously. Half way through the cooking time, add all the spices and the tomato purée and season to taste. Add a little water as necessary.

When the meat is browned, remove and keep warm in a covered serving dish in the oven.

Meanwhile prepare all the optional toppings and present in serving dishes at the table.

Just before serving, warm the hard corn shells in the oven and serve at the table.

BOBOTIE

In 1990 my future wife and I completed our MBA degree at Durham University. We had just finished the course, the Summer and Autumn lay in front of us, and so did a very large Mills mountain of debt! Just to help things along, we booked to go to Africa for six weeks and on our return we were shortly due to travel to our new life in West Yorkshire. So we flew to South Africa and Zimbabwe in October 1990 and holidayed there for six weeks. We had a brilliant and unforgettable time. We also tried South Africa's national dish – Bobotie – and I wrote down the recipe (see below). I have cooked it quite regularly ever since. Some recipes use beef mince but this is not right, the Cape recipe is made with minced turkey and that is what I always use.

RECIPE

Serves 4
Preparation Time – 30 minutes
Cooking Time – 60 minutes

WINE PAIRING

South African only please

INGREDIENTS

2 slices of white bread
275ml whole milk
2 tbsp vegetable oil
2 onions chopped quite fine
2 garlic cloves peeled and chopped
750g minced turkey
2 tbsps medium or hot curry powder
50g blanched almonds
75g sultanas
1 tbsp fresh chopped parsley
1 lemon, juice and grated rind
3 tbsp mango chutney
2 eggs, beaten

METHOD

Preheat the oven to 180°C. Grease a shallow baking dish. Using a separate non-metallic bowl soak the bread in the milk.

Heat the oil in a heavy based pan and fry the onion and garlic on medium heat for 5 minutes. Stir in the mince, breaking it up finely until well browned. Stir in the curry powder, almonds, sultanas, parsley, lemon juice and rind, mango chutney and season well with salt and pepper.

Remove the bread from the milk, squeezing back any excess milk. Mix the bread into the fried mince and then beat the eggs into the remaining milk in the bowl.

Spoon the mince mixture into the greased baking dish and level the top by dragging a fork across. Pour over the egg and milk mixture evenly and bake for 40 minutes until set and golden brown on top. Serve with a mixed salad and a good Cape wine!

BUTTER CHICKEN DELHI STYLE

Globally, this is probably the best known curry dish and originated from Old Delhi in the 1950s and is now a staple dish in many restaurants worldwide. Traditionally, it would be cooked in a tandoor oven but using a barbecue or griddle pan is a perfectly good alternative. The spiced butter sauce and chopped fresh red onion, chilli pepper and coriander are an excellent accompaniment and it is best served with rice and naan bread for a delicious meal.

RECIPE

Serves 4
Preparation Time – 30 minutes
Cooking Time – 40 minutes

WINE PAIRING

Pinot noir, Côtes du Rhône

INGREDIENTS

Marinade

80g greek yoghurt
2 tbsp lemon juice
1 tbsp grated, fresh root ginger
3 garlic cloves, crushed
2 tbsp medium hot chilli powder
1 tbsp curry powder
1 tbsp garam masala
1 tbsp turmeric
4 boneless chicken breasts or thighs, skinned

Curry Sauce

600g skinned, de-seeded tomatoes, finely chopped
3 tbsp vegetable oil
4 garlic cloves, crushed
1 tbsp grated, fresh root ginger
2 bay leaves
1 tbsp garam masala
4 cardamom pods, crushed
1 tbsp ground cloves
1 tbsp chilli powder
50g butter
1 green chilli, de-seeded and finely chopped
6 leaves fenugreek
50ml single cream

Spiced Butter

50g butter
2 tsp black mustard seeds
6 curry leaves

To Serve

½ red onion chopped
2 red chillis, de-seeded and finely chopped
Small bunch of coriander

METHOD

Thoroughly mix together the ground spices, yoghurt and lemon juice in a bowl for the marinade. Cut the chicken into bite size pieces and coat with the marinade. Cover and refrigerate for at least an hour, preferably overnight.

Heat the barbecue to approx. 250°C and arrange the marinated chicken pieces on the griddle plate and bake for approx. 15 minutes turning two or three times to ensure the pieces are cooked to a golden colour all over.

Meanwhile, start on the sauce by adding the tomatoes to a large pan together with the ginger, garlic, cardamom and bay leaves. Cook on medium heat for 20 minutes. Allow to cool slightly, remove the solid spices and whizz with a blender until smooth. Move to a fresh pan and add the chilli powder and cook on medium heat for 10 minutes.

Now add the chicken pieces and blend in the butter and cook on for 5-6 minutes. Add the ginger, green chilli and cream and cook for a few minutes more.

Add the fenugreek leaves and garam masala and check seasoning and heat gently for 2-3 minutes.

In a separate pan, add all the spiced butter ingredients and heat until the mustard seeds start popping.

Serve the curry over rice with the spiced butter and naan bread and the red onion, chillis and coriander scattered over the top. You could also add a small spoon of cream in the centre of each plate.

CHICKEN DOPIAZA

This has to be one of my favourite curry recipes. The chicken is marinated and precooked and best of all it features two helpings of onions, one in the main sauce and the other as a crispy garnish, hence 'dopiaza' – double onions. My version can be served with turmeric-laced rice and a nice fresh naan bread. Delicious!

RECIPE

Serves 4
Preparation Time – 15 minutes
Cooking Time – 60 minutes

WINE PAIRING

Lightly oaked chardonnay

INGREDIENTS

Marinade
1 tbsp ground coriander
1 tbsp ground cumin
2 tbsp hot curry powder
1 lime, zested and juiced
100g greek yoghurt
1 tbsp grated, fresh root ginger
3 garlic cloves, crushed
8 skinless, boneless chicken thighs, cut into bite sized pieces

Sauce
2 tbsp vegetable oil
3 large onions, finely chopped
300ml chicken stock
3 cardamom pods
1 tbsp local runny honey
400g skinned, deseeded tomatoes, chopped

To Serve
3 tbsp fresh coriander

METHOD

Thoroughly mix together half of the ground spices, the yoghurt, lime juice and zest with half of the garlic and ginger in a bowl for the marinade. Cut the chicken into bite size pieces and coat with the marinade. Cover and refrigerate for at least an hour, preferable overnight.

Start on the sauce by sautéeing half the onions in the oil on a medium heat for 10 minutes or so until caramelised adding a little stock if necessary. Then add the remaining garlic and ginger, about 2/3 of the remaining spices together with the cardamom and honey. Stir and cook for one minute then add the tomatoes and chicken stock, season and simmer for 20 minutes, stirring occasionally. Remove from the heat and set aside to cool slightly. Remove the solid spices and whizz the sauce with a blender until smooth.

Meanwhile, heat the barbecue to approx. 250°C and arrange the marinated chicken pieces on the griddle plate and bake for approx. 15 minutes turning two or three times to ensure the pieces are cooked to a golden colour all over.

Now add the chicken pieces to the pan containing the sauce, stir and cook on medium heat for approximately 10 to 12 minutes.

While this is cooking, make the second batch of onions. Take a fresh pan and a little oil and the rest of the onions and the remaining spices. Sauté for about 10 minutes on quite high heat until crispy and golden.

Serve the curry over rice with the naan bread and the fried onions and coriander scattered over the top.

CHICKEN KARAHI

Guess what? It's another curry! This dish originates from the Punjab and is cooked with green chillies and yoghurt. This recipe relies on marinating the chicken pieces in yoghurt and spices and pre-cooking in the oven prior to slow cooking. It is very simple to make and is one of my favourite curry dishes. A 'Karahi' is a heavy metal round dish with steep sides and handles, in which the food is traditionally cooked and served. I don't have one so I use a wok and slow cooker instead.

RECIPE

Serves 4
Preparation Time – 20 minutes + 60 minutes marinating time
Cooking Time – 2 hours

WINE PAIRING

Riesling, Sauvignon Blanc

INGREDIENTS

Marinade Mix
2 tbsp medium hot chilli powder
1 tbsp ground coriander
1 tbsp ground cumin
3 tbsp plain yoghurt

Chicken
3 tbsp vegetable oil
2 onions peeled and cut into large slices
4 garlic cloves, peeled
1 tbsp grated, fresh root ginger
4 boneless, skinless chicken breasts
3 tomatoes, chopped
6 green chillies, 2 of which finely chopped
200ml vegetable stock
Coriander leaves, torn to serve

METHOD

Thoroughly mix together the ground spices and yoghurt in a large bowl to complete the marinade mix and add the chicken, cut into bite size pieces and coat thoroughly with the marinade mix. Cover and put in the fridge for around 60 minutes.

Transfer the chicken pieces to a baking tray and bake in the oven for approx. 15-20 minutes.

Meanwhile, whizz the onion pieces and garlic through the grating attachment of a food blender to create a paste and add the grated ginger afterwards.

Then in a wok, fry the paste in the oil for approx. 7 minutes over medium heat, stirring regularly and then transfer the paste to the slow cooker on medium heat.

Transfer the baked chicken and the juices to the slow cooker and mix in the tomato pieces, the 2 finely chopped chillies and the vegetable stock.

Cook for 2 hours. Serve with rice, naans and garnish.

CHICKEN PROVENÇAL

This is the classic southern French casserole full of the local flavours of garlic, tomatoes, rosemary and olives. I enjoyed a few trips to France and this recipe is one of the things I brought back.

Make sure you use fresh herbs not dried, a good organic chicken and fresh, ripe vine tomatoes and reasonable French wine if you want it to taste something close to the version you might eat in southern France.

RECIPE

Serves 4
Preparation Time – 30 minutes
Cooking Time – 1½ hours

WINE PAIRING

A good Chardonnay should work OK or possibly a Sauvignon blanc, ideally the same wine that you used to make the dish

INGREDIENTS

1 organic chicken, jointed into 4 pieces
2 tbsp olive oil
1 large onion, finely chopped
1 green pepper, deseeded and cut into strips
500g vine tomatoes, halved
250g small button mushrooms
3 tbsp tomato purée
350ml white wine (half a bottle)
150ml water
16 black olives, pitted
A small bunch of rosemary, chopped
A few sprigs of thyme, basil and parsley all chopped

METHOD

Preheat the oven to 150°C.

In a large casserole dish, sauté the chicken pieces until golden and set aside. Now add the onion to the casserole dish and cook until browned.

Sir in the tomato purée and then add the wine and water. Return the chicken to the casserole with the vegetables, olives and all the herbs (reserving a small amount of the parsley for garnishing the dish when serving).

Cover the dish and put in the centre of the oven for 1½ hours, stirring occasionally and season to taste.

Garnish with the parsley and serve with French bread to mop up the juices.

CHICKEN SCHENKEL

I spent some years working with emergency services publications latterly as a book publisher and worked on a number of Fire Service books with varying degrees of success. I am very proud of some of the books, in particular those authored by Neil Wallington. Neil had spent his career in the Fire Service and had been Chief Fire Officer in Devon and certainly knew his stuff. We worked together on a number of books and one evening after work, over at his house in Lincolnshire, I was treated to this family recipe by Neil and his wife Susi.

RECIPE

Serves 4
Preparation Time – 25 minutes
Cooking Time – 45 minutes

WINE PAIRING

Light Chardonnay

INGREDIENTS

4 cooked chicken breasts cut into bite sized slices
2 heads of broccoli
2 x 400g cans of condensed chicken soup
200g mayonnaise
1 tbsp medium curry powder
1 lemon, zest and juice
250g cheddar, grated
100g breadcrumbs, toasted

METHOD

Pre-heat the oven to 180°C.

Pre-cook the chicken breasts in a steamer of salted water for approx. 15 minutes, run under cold water and cut into bite sized pieces.

In the meantime, heat up more salted water in a large pan and pre-cook the broccoli for 3 minutes.

Grease a large oven proof dish and add a layer of the chicken, then a layer of broccoli and then another layer of chicken. Season with salt and pepper.

Mix the soup, mayonnaise, curry powder, lemon zest and juice together and spread the mixture over the top of the chicken. Spread the cheese on top and finally sprinkle over the breadcrumbs.

Bake in the pre-heated oven for 45 minutes until lightly browned.

Serve immediately with a light salad.

CHICKEN TIKKA MASALA

The ubiquitous Chicken Tikka Masala is a 1970s classic and a great example of what is sometimes known as 'fusion cuisine'. For many people in Britain it was probably their first taste of Indian-style food in the 1970s. Chicken Tikka on its own is a northern Indian dish consisting of pieces of boneless chicken marinated in yoghurt and spices, cooked and served on a skewer, kebab-style often cooked in a 'Tandoor' oven, while Masala simply means a mixture of ground spices.

Chicken Tikka Masala was reputedly first prepared in the early 1970s by a Bangladeshi chef in Glasgow, who at the request of a customer, added a mild tomato and creamy sauce to his chicken tikka to replicate a Sunday Lunch-style 'Roast Chicken and Gravy'.

RECIPE

Serves 4
Preparation Time – 30 minutes
Plus minimum 2 hours marinading time
Cooking Time – 40 minutes

WINE PAIRING

Sparkling Rosé, Pinot Noir, Côtes du Rhône

INGREDIENTS

Spice Mix
2 tbsp medium hot chilli powder
1 tbsp paprika
1 tbsp ground coriander
1 tbsp ground cumin
1 tbsp turmeric
1 tsp ground cinnamon
1 tsp fenugreek

Chicken Tikka
⅔ of spice mix
3 tbsp plain yoghurt
2 tbsp lemon juice
1 tbsp grated, fresh root ginger
3 garlic cloves, crushed
4 boneless chicken breasts, skinned
Fresh coriander, torn to garnish

Curry Sauce
3 tbsp vegetable oil
2 onions, finely chopped
4 garlic cloves, crushed
1 tbsp grated, fresh root ginger
3 tbsp tomato purée
⅓ of spice mix
3 tbsp plain yoghurt

METHOD

Thoroughly mix together the ground spices in a small bowl to complete the spice mix.

For the chicken tikka, cut the chicken into bite sizes pieces and place in a large, non-metallic bowl. Season with salt and add the lemon juice and toss the chicken pieces.

Mix together the spice mix, ginger, garlic and yoghurt. Pour over the chicken and mix thoroughly. Cover and place in the fridge to marinate for a few hours or overnight if possible.

For the curry sauce, heat the oil in a large saucepan or wok and add the onion, garlic and ginger. Cook on a low/medium heat for approx. 10 minutes, stirring regularly with a wooden spoon and then a further 5 minutes on a slightly higher heat to brown lightly.

Add the remaining spice mix and tomato purée. Season with salt flakes and freshly ground black pepper and approx. 200ml of water. Bring to the boil, turn down the heat and simmer gently for 5 minutes.

Allow to cool a little and then blitz with a stick blender or in a jug blender until completely smooth and then stir in the yoghurt. This can be stored in the fridge for a few days or used straight away.

To cook the chicken, heat a griddle pan on high and then place the marinated chicken pieces on the griddle, having first wiped off any excess marinade. Cook until char lines appear and then turn over as necessary until the chicken is just cooked through. Repeat in batches as necessary and put the cooked chicken pieces in a large saucepan or wok.

Add the curry sauce and cook on low/medium heat and simmer for 10 minutes. Serve with torn, fresh coriander and lemon juice on top accompanied by rice and/or naan bread as desired.

CHILLI CON CARNE

Chilli con carne (Chili with meat), originated from northern Mexico and southern Texas. Small, informal restaurants, 'Chilli joints', starting popping up in the United States early in the 20th century. Quite when this dish properly arrived in the UK is not so certain, but it appears to have become popular in Britain by 1973 which is around the time when my Mother first cooked it at home. She made hers the Texan way with minced beef as opposed to the Mexican way with chopped beef and that's how I still make my version.

RECIPE

Serves 4
Preparation Time – 20 minutes
Cooking Time – 60 minutes

WINE PAIRING

Côtes du Rhône, Tempranillo, Zinfandel

INGREDIENTS

1 large onion, chopped
1 red pepper, chopped
3 garlic cloves, minced
2 tbsp vegetable oil
1 tbsp hot chilli powder
1 tbsp paprika
1 tsp ground cumin
500g lean, minced beef
300ml beef stock
1 tsp muscovado sugar (or small piece of dark chocolate)
3 tbsp tomato purée
400g tin of kidney beans
300g long grain rice
Soured cream and parsley to serve

METHOD

Prepare the vegetables ready for cooking and heat the oil in a large pan over medium heat. Add the onion and cook for about 5 minutes until translucent, stirring frequently.

Introduce the red pepper and garlic and continue cooking for a further 2 minutes. Now add all the spices, stir and cook for a further 3 minutes before transferring the contents to a bowl.

Add more oil to the pan and crumble in the minced beef using a wooden spatula to break it up finely. Continue cooking until the mince is browned and very granular.

Add back the vegetable mixture to the pan together with the beef stock, sugar and tomato purée and season with salt flakes and freshly ground black pepper. Mix well and bring to the boil and then simmer for 20 minutes, stirring regularly adding a little more water if necessary.

Then add the kidney beans and bring to the boil again. Simmer gently for about 20 minutes or until the mixture thickens.

Serve with rice and a dollop of soured cream and fresh parsley scattered on top.

COD WITH CHORIZO AND BEANS

This recipe uses the contrast of white flaky fish with spicy chorizo sausage to give it plenty of flavour and the addition of tomatoes, olives and courgettes to give it texture. It is a quite low calorie dish coming in at under 500 calories per portion, but it doesn't taste like it and is quite filling with the butter beans.

Unfortunately, when I cooked this recipe we bought the cod from the Co-op (no fishmongers left where we live) and it came in black plastic trays vacuum packed, two fillets per pack. This seems really ridiculous and the supermarkets should be told to stop supplying produce in excessive plastic packaging. I don't want their plastic trays which I have to pay for presumably, then have to put it in the garbage and pay for that and then pollute the planet for future generations. I am quite happy to have my fish and meat supplied in waxed paper wrappers which can be put in recycling and which are biodegradable. That's my moan out of the way, good luck finding your cod fillets more sympathetically wrapped.

RECIPE

Serves 4
Preparation Time – 15 minutes
Cooking time – 30 minutes

WINE PAIRING

A light red such as a Pinot Noir

INGREDIENTS

2 tbsp olive oil
2 medium courgettes, thickly sliced
4 garlic cloves, peeled and thickly sliced
150ml fish stock
250g on the vine cherry tomatoes
50g pitted black or green olives
400g butter beans
4 cod fillets, each around 150g
20 thinly sliced chorizo sausage
1 lemon, zested and juiced
3 tbsp chopped parsley

METHOD

Pre-heat the oven to 180°C. Grease a large ovenproof dish or baking tray with the olive oil. Add the courgette slices, sprinkle on the garlic and pour in half the fish stock and season with salt and pepper. Bake in the pre-heated oven for 15 minutes.

Remove the dish from the oven and scatter on the butter beans. Then place the 4 cod fillets in each quarter of the dish and press in slightly. Scatter in the olives and tomatoes next to the cod fillets and place 5 chorizo slices on top of each fish. Sprinkle over the lemon zest and drip over the lemon juice and season as desired.

Bake for 15 minutes until the chorizo is well cooked and the cod is just cooked. Divide between plates with a spatula for the fish and vegetables and a spoon for the juices and then garnish with the parsley.

CURRIED SHEPHERD'S PIE

I have just started making this recipe. Whilst writing this book it got me thinking a bit more about cooking styles, what type of cooking we make at different times of life and how cookery has changed in recent times. It occurred to me that many successful British meals have a mixture of comfort food from one culture or a mix of different cultural backgrounds. Many of the recipes which contain influences from more than one culture can be skewed in favour of one culture rather than another. I think this one mixes English and Indian cultures very evenly with common ingredients which are spiced, cooked and presented differently to the way in which each culture traditionally presents its recipes and ingredients.

My recipe contains Rogan Josh spice mix, minced beef, home grown potatoes, celery and carrots and is inexpensive, ideal served with fresh salad, lasts in the fridge and can be frozen too. So here it is - Curried Shepherd's Pie!

RECIPE

Serves 4
Preparation Time – 30 minutes
Cooking Time – 60 minutes

WINE PAIRING

Light red such as Pinot Noir

INGREDIENTS

Rogan Josh Spice Mix
1 tbsp paprika
1 btsp ground cumin
1 tbsp ground coriander
1 tbsp turmeric
1 tbsp garam masala
1 tbsp black pepper, ground
1 tbsp red cayenne pepper
2 tbsp tomato purée
1 tbsp red chilli paste

Meat Mixture
2 tbsp olive oil
1 large onion, finely chopped
2 medium carrots, peeled and finely chopped
2 celery sticks, strings removed, finely chopped
3 garlic cloves, peeled and finely chopped
500g lean beef mince
3 tbsp tomato purée (or 1 large ripe tomato, chopped)
1 beef stock cube

Topping
2kg white potatoes
50ml milk
Large knob of butter
2 tbsp ground turmeric

METHOD

Preheat oven to 180°C.

Heat 2 tbsp olive oil in a large saucepan or wok on low to medium heat and add the onions, carrots, celery and garlic, and cook for 10 minutes, stirring regularly.

Increase the heat to medium and add the beef mince, breaking it up and stirring constantly. Add all the Rogan Josh spice mix ingredients and cover and simmer for 20 minutes, adding water and seasoning as required.

Meanwhile, peel and chop the potatoes and cook for 20 minutes on a medium heat. Check the potatoes are cooked through and add the turmeric, butter and milk. Mash thoroughly.

Now assemble the recipe in a baking dish by scooping the curried meat into the dish, levelling it out and then arranging the mashed potatoes on top. Level and brush a fork over the surface to give an uneven finish.

Bake in the oven for 30-40 minutes until the potato is golden on top.

Allow to rest a little (and the recipe too!) and then serve with a salad or vegetable accompaniment.

KEEMA CURRY WITH POTATOES AND GREEN BEANS

In 2020 we travelled to Canada in August as we have done for many years and went to stay at the Cottage on Georgian Bay for two weeks in self isolation. This meant that other family members did the food shopping for our stay and left it at the Cottage. We flew from Manchester on the Thursday morning before West Yorkshire and Greater Manchester were locked down, so got out just in time. We took the KLM flight to Amsterdam and then connected to the Toronto flight. On arrival we went through immigration and customs before picking up a car that was delivered to the airport by my Father-in-Law and drove the 100 miles or so up to the marina at Hidden Glen at the edge of Georgian Bay, just as the sun was setting.

We transferred our luggage to the boat and power boated the six mile water journey to the Cottage arriving just as darkness was descending. A good thing too as boating at night is not fun, when all the islands look the same and it is difficult to spot familiar landmarks. Not knowing quite what the situation would be like for food and drink when we arrived, back in England I had packed a full spice set for curries and a litre of gin in my luggage, so I was well prepared. The first night we were tired and it was very late so we ate leftover airline food (yuk!) but the second night, after a beautiful sunny day, I cooked and served this recipe and we ate *al fresco* on the deck and witnessed an amazing sunset, a Keema Curry sunset!

RECIPE

Serves 4
Preparation Time – 20 minutes
Cooking Time – 30 minutes

WINE PAIRING

Chardonnay or a light red such as Beaujolais

INGREDIENTS

2 tbsp vegetable oil
1 onion, chopped
1 tbsp grated, fresh root ginger
1 red chilli pepper, chopped and de-seeded
4 garlic cloves, chopped
2 tbsp medium curry powder
1 tbsp chilli powder
500g minced beef
2 tbsp tomato purée
250ml beef stock
750g new potatoes
250g fresh green beans

METHOD

In a heavy pan fry the onions, ginger, garlic and chilli pepper in vegetable oil over medium heat for approx. 5 minutes until lightly browned at the edges, stirring constantly. Set aside in a separate bowl to cool slightly.

Add the potatoes to another saucepan of cold water and bring to the boil and simmer for approx. 10 minutes. Use a sharp pointed knife and test that it slides easily through the potatoes to make sure they are adequately cooked.

Using the same heavy pan used for the onions, add the minced beef and sauteé for approximately 10 minutes, gradually browning the mince. Add the spices, cooked potatoes, beef stock, seasoning and tomato purée and simmer for 5 minutes.

Then add the green beans and continue cooking until the beans are cooked through, approximately 5 minutes.

Serve the curry on a bed of boiled rice with naan bread.

KERALAN MALABAR PRAWNS

I have only stayed in India once and that was with work. I stayed in the southern city of Bangalore in Karnataka state and was entertained and hosted by my friends Mr. Ram Jalan and Mr. Sankaran. I really enjoyed my visit and was able to enjoy plenty of South Indian cooking including lots of dhosas and South Indian beer! It is a shame there is not much tradition of this southern indian style of cooking in the UK but here is a taste of what you are missing from Kerala state which specialises in fish and seafood dishes.

RECIPE
Serves 4
Preparation Time – 15 minutes
Cooking time – 15 minutes

WINE PAIRING
Lightly oaked chardonnay

INGREDIENTS
400g raw king prawns
3 tbsp hot chilli powder
1 tbsp turmeric
1 lemon, juiced and zested
40g fresh ginger, half grated, half sliced and chopped
1 tbsp vegetable oil
4 curry leaves
3 green chillis, chopped and deseeded
1 medium onion, chopped
1 tsp cracked black pepper

Garnish
40g fresh coconut, grated
Small bunch fresh coriander, torn

METHOD
Wash the king prawns in cold water and pat dry. Place in a bowl and add the chilli powder, turmeric, lemon juice and grated ginger. Mix thoroughly, cover and set aside.

Heat the oil in a large saucepan or wok and add the curry leaves, green chillis and onion and cook gently until translucent, approximately 8 minutes.

Add the cracked black pepper and then the prawns and cook on medium heat for about 5 minutes until all the prawns are cooked through.

Serve the prawns and the juices with the coconut and torn coriander sprinkled on top.

LAMB ROGAN JOSH

This curry dish has a fresh spice mix which can be prepared in advance and stored in the fridge. Rogan Josh is an aromatic curried meat dish which originates from Persia and Kashmir and is usually made with a red meat such as lamb or goat, but in Britain chicken and beef are also used. My version uses cubed lamb and is cooked in a slow cooker to allow the lamb to become tender.

RECIPE

Serves 4
Preparation Time – 20 minutes
Cooking Time – 2 hours

WINE PAIRING

Viognier or a light red such as Beaujolais or Pinot Noir

INGREDIENTS

Curry Paste
1 tbsp paprika
1 btsp ground cumin
1 tbsp ground coriander
1 tbsp turmeric
1 tbsp garam masala
1 tbsp black pepper
1 tbsp red cayenne pepper
2 tbsp tomato purée
1 tbsp red chilli paste

Curry
2 tbsp vegetable oil
500g cubed lamb
1 onion, roughly chopped
1 tbsp grated, fresh root ginger
3 garlic cloves, crushed
6 cardamom pods lightly crushed
1 tbsp ground cinnamon
1 tbsp ground cloves
6 tbsp plain Yoghurt
Fresh coriander, torn (to serve)

METHOD

Mix the spices for the paste and either use straight away or store in a jar in the fridge, or both if you make double.

Add the tomato and red chilli to the spice mix and blend with a small spoon and set aside.

Mix the lamb and onions with the ground cinnamon, cloves and cardamom pods in a heavy pan or wok. Cook on medium heat for 5 minutes add the ginger and garlic and cook for a further 3 minutes stirring constantly. Add the spice paste and cook for a further 3 minutes.

Now transfer the lamb mix to the slow cooker and set to medium heat. Add around 200ml of water to the mix, stir and cover with the slow cooker lid on for 90 minutes, stirring occasionally.

Add the yoghurt to the slow cooker and stir through, cooking for a further 30 minutes.

Now, prepare the rice and serve the curry on a bed of rice with torn coriander leaves on top.

MEATBALL BLACK BEAN CHILLI

This recipe is an excellent alternative to the standard variety made with minced beef and kidney beans. This recipe is much easier to make and quicker to cook with the fried meatballs and tasty small black beans a welcome change.

RECIPE

Serves 4
Preparation Time – 10 minutes
Cooking Time – 30 minutes

WINE PAIRING

Californian Zinfandel

INGREDIENTS

450g lean, minced beef, formed into meatballs
1 large onion, chopped
1 red pepper, chopped
3 garlic cloves, minced
2 tbsp vegetable oil
1 tbsp hot chilli powder
1 tbsp paprika
2 tsp ground cumin
200ml beef stock
400g tin of black beans, drained and rinsed
400g fresh tomatoes, skins removed, de-seeded and chopped
300g long grain rice, rinsed
Torn coriander leaves to serve

METHOD

Divide the beef mince into four equal portions and roll each portion into four meatballs to make 16 in total. Season with half the chilli powder, paprika and cumin and some salt and pepper.

Heat half the oil in a large frying pan and sauté the meatballs over medium high heat for 5-7 minutes, tossing frequently so that they brown all over. Remove the meatballs from the heat and tip into a large saucepan.

Add the remaining olive oil to the frying pan, add the onion, red pepper and garlic and cook for about 5 minutes until translucent, stirring frequently.

Remove from the heat and tip into the large saucepan with the meatballs.

Now add all the remaining spices, the beef stock, black beans and tomatoes. Stir and cook on medium heat for a further 15 minutes covered.

Meanwhile cook the rice in salted water according to pack instructions.

Serve the meatball chilli on top of the rice with the coriander scattered on top.

MOUSSAKA

Moussaka was a regular dish in our house in the 1970s and was almost as popular as sausage casserole or ratatouille. Mass tourism to Greek islands had just begun and warm retsina was in vogue (I gave up in 1982 after a nasty experience on the beach in Ibiza). Nana Mouskouri and Demis Roussos were on the wireless and a good bit of plate smashing was in fashion, especially in our house! Moussaka seemed the ideal spring/summer dish with ingredients we were comfortable with (minced lamb, tomatoes, onion and garlic), but with the added Mediterranean ingredient of aubergines and a creamy baked topping.

RECIPE
Serves 4
Preparation Time – 30 minutes
Cooking Time – 40 minutes

WINE PAIRING
Tempranillo or Sangiovese

INGREDIENTS
3 large aubergines, sliced
4-6 tbsp vegetable oil
1 large onion, chopped
3 garlic cloves, crushed
500g minced lamb
400g tin, chopped tomatoes
3 tbsp tomato purée
25g unsalted butter
25g plain flour
300ml fresh milk
1 egg, beaten

METHOD
Place the aubergine slices in a large colander and sprinkle generously with salt. Set aside for 20 minutes to draw out the bitter juices.

Heat half of the oil in a large heavy based pan or wok and gently fry the onion and garlic for 5 minutes.

Add the minced lamb, breaking it up with a wooden spatula and stir regularly until browned.

Add the tomatoes, tomato purée and seasoning and bring to the boil, then cover and simmer for 20 minutes.

Pre-heat the oven to 200°C.

Drain the aubergines, rinse with cold water and dry on a clean kitchen towel or kitchen paper. Fry the aubergine slices in batches in a pan with the remaining oil until golden.

Arrange a layer of aubergines in a greased oven proof dish, cover with half the mince, then repeat and finish with a third layer of aubergines.

Melt the butter in a pan, stir in the flour gradually and bring to the boil, stirring until thick. Season, remove from the heat and stir in the beaten egg.

Spoon the sauce over the aubergines and bake in the oven for 40 minutes until browned.

Serve with a greek or garden salad.

MUTTON KOFTAS

Koftas are one of my favourite meals, reminiscent of late night kebabs after a few beers, they are primarily a Middle Eastern dish. They are pleasantly spiced and meaty and are best accompanied by pitta or flatbreads, salad and yoghurt.

RECIPE

Serves 4
Preparation Time – 30 minutes
Cooking Time – 40 minutes

WINE PAIRING

Dry Sauvignon Blanc

INGREDIENTS

Koftas
1 large onion, chopped
4 garlic cloves, peeled and sliced
600g minced lamb
3 cm piece of ginger, peeled and finely grated
1 tbsp ground cumin
1 tbsp ground coriander
1 tbsp garam masala
300ml plain yoghurt
4 tbsp vegetable oil
4 cardamom pods, lightly crushed
4 cloves

Accompaniments to serve
8 large pitta pockets, sliced open
small head of lettuce, shredded
8 tbsp diced cucumber pieces
1 red pepper, sliced
plain yoghurt
fresh mint, torn to garnish
lemon wedges

METHOD

Gently fry the onion and garlic for 5 minutes to soften over medium heat in a large frying pan with half the oil.

In a mixing bowl, mix the minced lamb with the dried spices, the ginger and the onion and garlic. Add 2 tbsp of yoghurt and form into 16 sausage shaped koftas.

Heat the remaining the oil in the frying pan and add the cardamom pods and cloves for around 30 seconds. Now, add the koftas and brown on all sides.

Add the remaining yoghurt together with 150ml of water. Bring to the boil, cover and simmer for around 30 minutes or until all the liquid has been absorbed.

Remove the koftas onto a serving dish and serve at the table with the accompaniments for diners to make up their own pitta pockets with koftas and salad.

OSSOBUCCO

A great, traditional Italian recipe, it's a veal stew really, slow cooked in wine and vegetables and probably best suited to the colder winter months. What makes it memorable for me is the citrus garnish with chopped parsley that gives it a lift and a fresh taste that goes well with the stewed meat. Traditionally, it is served with creamed or mashed potatoes.

RECIPE

Serves 4
Preparation Time – 25 minutes
Cooking Time   1 hour 30 minutes

WINE PAIRING

Barolo or other strong red

INGREDIENTS

1kg ossobucco (veal shin)
2 tbsp olive oil
1 onion, finely chopped
1 large carrot, finely chopped
2 celery sticks, finely chopped
2 ripe tomatoes, peeled, deseeded and chopped
2 tbsp plain flour
400ml vegetable stock
1 glass white wine
3 tbsp parsley, chopped
3 tbsp rosemary, chopped
2 bay leaves

For The Garnish

1 lemon, grated zest of
1 orange, grated zest of
3 tbsp parsley, chopped

METHOD

Fry the chopped vegetables in oil over a light heat for 3 minutes and set aside.

Coat the ossobucco with flour and seasoning and fry on a medium heat until golden all over.

Combine the ossobucco and vegetables in a large pan or in a slow cooker and add the herbs and stock. Use the wine to deglaze the ossobucco frying pan and add this to the large pan.

Cover and cook over a low heat for approximately one hour.

Meanwhile prepare the mashed potatoes about 30 minutes before the end of the stew cooking time and chop and combine the garnish ingredients.

Serve on plates with dollops of mashed potatoes and the ossobucco and sauce on top and the garnish sprinkled over.

POLLO FAJITAS

In Tex-Mex and Mexican cuisine a fajita is a grilled meat dish usually served as a taco on a flour or corn tortilla. It is a relatively quick and easy meal to make, ideal for families with teenage children who are happy with the level of spices and like that they can roll up the tortilla into a tube shape, fold over the base and eat it with their hands like a sandwich.

RECIPE

Serves 4
Preparation Time – 20 minutes
Cooking Time – 20 minutes

WINE PAIRING

Red – Zinfandel, White – Chardonnay or Gewürztraminer

INGREDIENTS

4 chicken breasts cut into bite sized slices
2 red onions, peeled and sliced
2 red peppers, cored and sliced
2 red chilli peppers, deseeded and finely chopped

Marinade
2 tbsp ground coriander
2 tbsp smoked paprika
1 tsp ground cumin
4 garlic cloves, crushed
6 tbsp olive oil
2 limes, rind grated and juiced
1 tsp Tabasco sauce

To Serve
8 medium tortillas (1 packet normally)
Mixed salad
Large jar of fresh Salsa

METHOD

Preheat the oven to 150°C.

Mix all the marinade ingredients in a large non-metallic bowl and add the chicken, onions, red peppers and red chilli peppers. Mix ensuring everything is coated in the marinade.

Heat a large griddle pan to high and sauté the chicken and vegetable mixture, turning frequently with a wooden spatula or tongs for approx. 5 minutes. You may need to repeat this in batches. Check the chicken is cooked through and if necessary transfer batches to a casserole dish and place in the oven.

5 minutes before serving, wrap the tortillas in tin foil and heat in the oven.

Serve the chicken and vegetable mixture on top of each tortilla and accompany with the salsa and the mixed salad.

PORK STEAK WITH CREAMY BLUE CHEESE RELISH

A very tasty recipe with a combination of the pork flavours set off against the creamy cheese relish. The lean pork steaks should be cut fairly thick, around 1 to 1 ½ inches. This allows you to barbecue on a high heat and sear the outers with nice grill marks, but ensures the steaks do not dry out while cooking. You will probably need 8-10 minutes cooking on each side and then you need to let the steaks rest for a further 5 minutes before serving. The steaks would best be served with freshly dug, steamed new potatoes from the garden and a crunchy fresh green salad.

RECIPE

Serves 4
Preparation Time – 5 minutes
Cooking Time – 20 minutes

WINE PAIRING

Pinot Noir or Zinfandel

INGREDIENTS

4 lean pork loin steaks each approx. 150g
4 tbsp low fat fromage frais
50g blue cheese like Stilton, crumbled
2 spring onions, finely chopped

METHOD

Preheat the barbecue to 250°C with the lid on.

Barbecue steaks for desired time, turning once only and allow to rest.

Mix all the sauce ingredients together.

Serve the steaks with the sauce on top with the new potatoes and a green salad to the side.

PAELLA

Paella is one of Spain's best recognised dishes and a favourite of British holidaymakers at Spanish coastal resorts. Traditionally from the Valencia region, paella was made with chicken or rabbit (and even snails) but no seafood. The version below is a lot more like the modern versions and features chorizo, chicken and king prawns. For parties or large gatherings, paella is made in a large paella dish but a good sized lidded wok should be adequate.

RECIPE

Serves Four
Preparation Time – 30 minutes
Cooking Time – 45 minutes

WINE PAIRING

Tempranillo

INGREDIENTS

Large pinch of saffron
500ml chicken stock
3 tbsp olive oil
150g chorizo, sliced quite thinly
400g skinless, boneless chicken thighs, chopped into bite sized pieces
1 large onion, finely chopped
1 red pepper, deseeded and finely chopped
3 garlic cloves, finely chopped
2 tbsp vegetable oil
1 tbsp paprika
250g paella/risotto rice
4 ripe tomatoes, skinned, deseeded and chopped
100g freshly podded or frozen peas
250g raw king prawns, heads and shell removed (if desired)

To Serve
Small bunch flat leaf parsley, chopped
1 lemon cut into wedges

METHOD

Submerge the saffron in the chicken stock and leave to infuse. Heat one tablespoon of the oil in a large lidded saucepan, paella dish or wok and fry the chorizo slices on medium heat for 3 minutes or until crisp. Remove and set aside, leaving the infused oil in the pan.

Now add the chicken pieces to the pan and cook on high heat for 8 minutes or until cooked through and set aside. Add a further splash of oil to the pan and sauté the onion and garlic for about 5 minutes until translucent, stirring frequently.

Now add the red pepper, paprika, rice and the remaining oil. Stir and cook on medium for 5 minutes. Add the stock, scraping up browned pieces from the bottom of the pan. Return the chicken to the pan, cover and cook on medium heat for 10 minutes.

Stir a little and add the chorizo, prawns and peas on the surface and replace the lid and cook for a further 6-8 minutes ensuring that the prawns turn pink and are cooked through and the rice is also cooked through.

Allow to rest for 5 minutes, covered, then serve scattered with parsley over the top and accompanied by lemon wedges.

SPAGHETTI BOLOGNESE

'Spag Bol' as it is known (certainly in our house) is a well-known international dish. It originates from Bologna in Italy. When we stayed in Bologna the sauce or ragù was usually served with a flat pasta such as tagliatelle or fettucine. Like many international dishes, it utilises the best and most local prolific ingredients of its origins in this case beef mince, fresh tomatoes, pasta and parmesan cheese.

RECIPE

Serves 4
Preparation Time – 30 minutes
Cooking Time – 1¼ hours

WINE PAIRING

Nero d'Avola, Chianti Classico, Primitivo or even Barolo

INGREDIENTS

Meat
2 tbsp olive oil
6 rashers back bacon
1 large onion, finely chopped
2 medium carrots, peeled and finely chopped
2 celery sticks, strings removed and finely chopped
3 garlic cloves, peeled and finely chopped
500g lean beef mince
200g small, white button mushrooms (optional)

Sauce
2 x 400g tins chopped tomatoes
2 tsp dried oregano
3 fresh bay leaves
3 tbsp tomato purée
1 beef stock cube
125ml Italian red wine, (see wine pairing)
12 small vine or cherry tomatoes quartered

To Serve
300g fresh spaghetti
100g parmesan, grated

METHOD

Heat 1 tbsp olive oil in a large saucepan or wok on medium heat and fry the bacon rashers, chopped into bite sized pieces, until browned.

Add the onions, carrots, celery and garlic, reduce the heat and cook for 10 minutes, stirring regularly.

Increase the heat to medium and add the beef mince, breaking it up and stirring constantly. Add all the sauce ingredients, well mixed in and bring to the boil. Cover and simmer for 1 hour, seasoning as required.

Near the end of the cooking time prepare the pasta as required.

Serve the meat and ragú mix over a bed of spaghetti and grate the parmesan over the top with freshly grated black pepper.

STRIPLOIN STEAK WITH HOT TOMATO SAUCE

An excellent recipe for summer evenings and a good one to do on the barbecue. The striploin steak comes from the short loin of the cow. It features a muscle, the *longissimus* (honestly!) that does very little work, resulting in a particularly tender meat. Make sure you have your steaks cut thick, around 1 ½ to 2 inches. This allows you to barbecue on a high heat and sear the outers with nice grill marks, but leave the centres rare and pink. You will probably need 3-4 minutes cooking on each side and then you need to let the steaks rest for a further 3 minutes before serving. This chilli tomato sauce recipe makes a welcome change to shop-bought sauces. Home fries would be an excellent accompaniment with a fresh green salad.

RECIPE

Serves 4
Preparation Time – 5 minutes
Cooking Time – 15 minutes

WINE PAIRING

Cabernet Sauvignon

INGREDIENTS

- 4 striploin steaks each 100 – 200g, dependent on greed v cost ratio
- 4 tbsp low fat fromage frais
- 2 ripe tomatoes, skinned, de-seeded and finely chopped
- 1 tbsp hot chilli powder
- 2 red chilli peppers, chopped finely and de-seeded

METHOD

Preheat the barbecue to 250°C with the lid on. Barbecue steaks for desired time, turning once only.

Mix all the sauce ingredients together.

Serve the steaks with a dollop of the sauce on top with the home fries and green salad at the side.

SWEET AND SOUR CHICKEN

Out with the wok (and numerous other bowls and pans) for this 1980s takeaway delight! Sweet and sour dishes originate from the Canton region of China but are now found in most countries in some form or other including this version. The Chinese generally pair certain types of sauces with particular meats. Sweet and sour sauces are synonymous with chicken and pork, and are normally made by mixing sugar or honey with vinegar, soy sauce and spices such as ginger or chilli. The sauce can be used as a dipping sauce for meat and fish or can be added to the wok shortly before serving. There are significant variations in sweet and sour sauces in different regions of China and many other nations too. The main ingredients of a sweet and sour dish are meat and the vegetables used are onions, red and green peppers and pineapple. The recipe below is served Hong Kong style, which involves the chicken pieces being dipped in whisked eggs, coated in cornflour and fried to provide a crispy coating prior to being added to the wok with the sauce near the end of cooking the main recipe.

RECIPE

Serves 4
Preparation Time – 30 minutes
Cooking Time – 45 minutes

WINE PAIRING

Riesling, Viognier

INGREDIENTS

Sweet and Sour Sauce
6 tbsp tomato ketchup
6 tbsp rice wine vinegar
4 tbsp runny honey
2 tbsp brown sugar
1 tbsp dark soy sauce
150ml vegetable stock
1 tbsp cornflour
Pinch of dried chilli flakes

Main Recipe
4 boneless, skinless chicken breasts cut into bite size pieces
2 eggs whisked
120g cornflour
2 tbsp vegetable oil
1 medium pineapple peeled, core removed and cut into bite sized pieces
1 large onion, peeled and cut into bite sized pieces
1 red pepper, washed, core removed and cut into bite sized pieces
1 green pepper, washed, core removed and cut into bite sized pieces

METHOD

Add all the sweet and sour sauce ingredients to a small pan and heat on a low heat until the sauce has thickened to a smooth consistency. Remove from the heat and set aside for the moment and move on to the main recipe.

Now the messy bit! Put out two bowls next to each other, the first containing the whisked eggs, the second the cornflour. Dip each of the chicken pieces in the egg mixture and then coat in the cornflour. I suggest using tongs and coating the chicken in batches, and make sure the *chef de plonge* is on duty!

Heat the oil in the wok to high and fry the coated chicken pieces (in batches) for approx. 5 minutes until lightly browned all over and then set aside and keep warm. Clean the wok and add more vegetable oil. Then fry the onion, peppers and pineapple on high heat for approx. 3 minutes.

Now add the reserved sweet and sour sauce and the pre-cooked chicken, reducing the heat to medium. Cook through quickly until bubbling gently and then serve with steamed rice.

SAGE STUFFED CHICKEN BREASTS

Fresh sage is a delicious and versatile herb loaded with antioxidants and we are lucky to have a vigorous plant growing in our garden. It has proved frost resistant here in northern England and can be picked year round and lasts well in the fridge. The sage butter for this recipe can be made and frozen for use at a later time.

RECIPE
Serves 4
Preparation Time – 30 minutes
Cooking Time – 30 minutes

WINE PAIRING
Viognier

INGREDIENTS
Sage Butter
15 fresh sage leaves
120g softened butter
1 tbsp wholegrain mustard

Main Recipe
4 boneless, skinless chicken breasts
8 rashers back bacon or prosciutto slices
2 tbsp olive oil

Sauce
1 medium glass of white wine
1 garlic clove crushed
3 fresh sage leaves

METHOD

Preheat the oven to 170°C. For the sage butter, finely chop 12 of the sage leaves and mix in with the butter, wholegrain mustard and freshly ground black pepper and salt. You could double this and freeze the second half.

Wash and dry the chicken breasts and either slice open a pocket or open the flap if there is one and insert a quarter of the sage butter mixture into each chicken breast. Using 2 bacon rashers for each breast, wrap around the chicken firmly to form a wrapper slightly overlapping each rasher with 1 overlap on each side of the breast.

Heat the olive oil in a heavy pan and add all 4 stuffed chicken breasts to the pan. On medium heat fry each side for approx. 4 minutes until lightly browned. Then move the chicken breasts to an ovenproof dish and bake in the preheated oven for 20 minutes.

Remove the chicken breasts from the pan, retaining the juices in the pan, and allow to rest for approx. 10 minutes. While the chicken is resting, make the sauce in the pan with the retained juices. Add the white wine, scrape the pan and cook on medium heat. Chop the remaining sage leaves and add to the pan with the crushed garlic. Season with salt and pepper and cook for a couple of minutes stirring constantly.

Serve the chicken breasts with mashed potato and pan fried courgettes and pour over the sauce.

TANDOORI CHICKEN WITH ROASTED SWEET POTATOES

An inexpensive meal that is easy to prepare, cooks in a single dish and is ready in an hour or so. This is a good late Spring meal as it is clean and fresh and the fresh mint in the garden will just be starting to grow in early to mid-May, so will be young and tender which is ideal for this dish and for the raita.

RECIPE
Serves 4
Preparation Time – 10 minutes
Cooking time – 60 minutes

WINE PAIRING
Pinot Noir or Beaujolais

INGREDIENTS
Main Dish
8 chicken thighs
2 large sweet potatoes, peeled and cut into 2 cm cubes
1 large red onion, cut into bite sized pieces
6 tbsp low fat natural yoghurt
1 tbsp olive oil
1 lemon zest and juice
5 garlic cloves, peeled and crushed
2 tbsp, fresh ginger, grated
1 tbsp ground cumin
1 tbsp ground turmeric
1 tbsp medium chilli powder
2 tbsp smoked paprika
1 tbsp garam masala

Raita
8 tbsp low fat natural yoghurt
½ cucumber, peeled and chopped
1 small red onion, peeled and roughly chopped
1 small mango, peeled, pitted and chopped
Handful of fresh mint, torn

METHOD
Pre-heat the oven to 180°C.

Put the chicken thighs, sweet potato and red onion pieces, spread out in a large oven proof dish or roasting tin.

In a medium sized bowl mix together the yoghurt, olive oil, lemon zest and juice, garlic, ginger, cumin, turmeric, chilli powder, half the paprika and season with salt and pepper. Spread this mixture evenly over the chicken and vegetables.

Scatter the chicken and vegetables with the remaining paprika and the garam masala and place in the middle of the pre-heated oven for 60 minutes.

Meanwhile, prepare the raita by mixing the red onion, cucumber and mango in a medium sized bowl and lightly coat with the yoghurt. Scatter some of the torn mint on top leaving the rest to scatter on the tray of chicken.

Take the chicken out of the oven and allow to rest for 5 minutes before serving with the raita and naans if desired and garnished with the remaining mint.

THIRTEEN MINUTE CORN

As a fairly frequent visitor to Ontario in the summer months I have witnessed the rituals surrounding corn on the cob. The corn grows quickly in the hot summer months in Ontario and August is the main harvesting month. It is said to be ready when the plants are 'as high as an elephant's eye'. It should be eaten as soon as possible after picking, in order to maintain its sweetness.

The most common way to prepare corn on the cob is to remove the husks and silks and plunge into boiling water. The corn cobs should be boiled, turning occasionally, for exactly 13 minutes! This recipe is the barbecue *au naturel* version from my brother-in-law Nicholas.

In this version, the husks are pre-soaked in salted cold water for approx. 2 hours. It is possible to fold back the husks and remove the silks prior to this if desired so that you don't have to do it after cooking. This soaking process ensures that the corn cobs have plenty of liquid which can help them to steam cook in their husks. The barbecue should be set to medium and the husks cooked for 16-20 minutes turning every 4 or 5 minutes to ensure equal cooking. After removing the husks the corn is ready to be rolled in butter, salted and eaten, either on its own or as an accompaniment to another dish or dishes.

RECIPE

Serves 4
Preparation/Soaking Time – 2 hours
Cooking Time – 20 minutes

WINE PAIRING

Anything you have to hand, corn is quite neutral in taste

INGREDIENTS

4 freshly picked corn husks
2 tbsp butter

METHOD

Fold back husks and remove silks from the corn cobs, fold back and immerse in very cold, salted water.

Preheat the barbecue to 200°C with the lid on.

Barbecue the corn husks for 16-20 minutes, turning regularly.

Remove from the heat and remove the husks and any remaining silks.

Roll in butter, season with salt and serve.

TREVIGIANA SPAGHETTI

This is a light and easy main course which can be prepared and cooked in under half an hour. This is spaghetti from Treviso with pancetta, rocket, eggs and parmesan, dusted with freshly ground black pepper and parmesan shavings. What's not to like?

RECIPE

Serves 4
Preparation Time – 10 minutes
Cooking time – 15 minutes

WINE PAIRING

Pinot noir or Sangiovese

INGREDIENTS

350g fresh spaghetti
100g pancetta cut into fine strips or cubes
4 egg yolks, beaten
2 tbsp olive oil
1 medium onion, chopped
1 handful rocket leaves
4 radicchio leaves, chopped
50g coarsely grated parmesan

METHOD

Heat a large pan of salted water and cook the spaghetti according to instructions.

Meanwhile, fry the chopped onion in olive oil over a medium heat in a large saucepan until lightly golden.

Now add the pancetta and cook on for a few minutes.

As soon as the pasta is cooked *al dente* drain and immediately tip into the saucepan.

Sauté with the radicchio, the rocket and half the parmesan for 2 minutes then add the beaten egg yolks and stir the mixture until the egg scrambles.

Serve straight away with seasoning and the remainder of the parmesan.

DESSERTS

PEAR TARTE TATIN

The recent acquisition of a cast iron tarte tatin dish, a type of oven proof frying pan which can be used to fry and to bake dishes, led me to try out a range of recipes. The traditional tarte tatin is prepared with apples, sugar, butter and a puff pastry base but this recipe calls for sweet pears instead with the addition of a few spicy ingredients. I suppose it ought to be called Tarte Tatin du Poires avec les Épices!

RECIPE

Serves 4

Preparation Time – 30 minutes
Cooking Time – 40 minutes

WINE PAIRING

Sauternes

INGREDIENTS

3 large pears, peeled, cored and halved length ways
30g butter at room temperature
50g caster sugar
4 star anise
1 tsp vanilla essence
1 tsp ground cloves
1 tsp freshly ground black pepper
150g ready-made puff pastry
Double cream or crème fraîche to serve

METHOD

Spread out the butter evenly over the base of the tarte tatin dish and coat with the sugar. Sprinkle over the cloves and black pepper and drip over the vanilla essence. Imagine how the tarte will be cut into 4 slices and place each of the star anise into the centre of each slice.

Arrange the pear halves evenly in the dish, cut sides uppermost.

Roll out the pastry on a floured surface until it is just slightly larger than the top of the tarte tatin dish and place on top of the dish and tuck inside the rim.

Place the pan over a medium heat and cook for 10 minutes.

Transfer the tarte tatin dish to an oven preheated to 200°C for 20 minutes or so, until the pastry on top is lightly browned.

Remove from the oven and let stand for 5 minutes. Place a serving plate face down on top of the dish and using oven gloves and/or tea towels, quickly turn the pan and serving plate over together so that the tarte turns out onto the plate pastry side down with the pear uppermost.

Slice and serve with the double cream or crème fraîche.

RASPBERRY SOUFFLÉ

This is not an easy one, at least not for me, but if you get it right it's a great way to use the frozen raspberry crop.

RECIPE

Serves 4
Preparation Time – 20 minutes
Cooking Time – 45 minutes

WINE PAIRING

Dessert wine like Moscato d'Asti

INGREDIENTS

The Soufflé
50g icing sugar
150g defrosted or fresh raspberries
1 lemon, grated and juiced
1 egg yoke
2 egg whites
pinch of salt
20g unsalted butter at room temperature
20g caster sugar

The Sauce
12 apricot halves, skin and pits removed
40g caster sugar
1 vanilla pod
25ml brandy

METHOD

Pre-heat the oven to 200°C.

Place the apricots, sugar and vanilla with 50ml of water in a saucepan and simmer for 30 minutes.

Remove the vanilla pod and purée the mixture in a blender. Add the brandy and set aside.

Now, blend 40g of the icing sugar, most of the raspberries (save 12 for decoration) and lemon juice in a food processor. Then add the egg yolk and blend for 30 seconds.

Place the egg whites and a pinch of salt in a bowl and whisk until it nearly peaks. Add the remaining icing sugar and beat in thoroughly.

Stir half of this into the raspberry mix and then fold in the remainder with a metal spoon.

Grease four small soufflé dishes with the butter and sprinkle with the caster sugar.

Fill the dishes with raspberry/egg mix and ensure that the surface is smooth. Gently ease the mixture away from the sides of the dishes with a knife. Decorate with the remaining raspberries slightly embedded.

Bake for 12 minutes in the pre-heated oven and serve immediately with the apricot brandy sauce.

TIRAMISÚ

When I visit a new restaurant I often order the special of the day or chef's recommendation and if neither of those appeal then I order a well-known dish or a menu standard as a way of gauging the quality of the restaurant.

In the case of Italian restaurants, a starter of Insalata Tricoloré or a dessert of Tiramisú is a good way of finding out more about the restaurant and as I always enjoy a really fresh preparation of either dish, there is also the expectation of possibly something special! This is my version of Tiramisú, made with strong, fresh americano coffee and some tasty amaretto. Some regions of Italy use other spirits instead of amaretto such as brandy or a liqueur.

RECIPE

Serves 4
Preparation Time – 30 minutes
Setting Time – 1 hour minimum in the fridge.

WINE PAIRING

The same liqueur you have used to make the recipe, in this case amaretto

INGREDIENTS

400g mascarpone
200ml double cream, whipped
5 tbsp caster sugar
4 egg yolks
200g sponge finger biscuits
4 tbsp amaretto
1 cup of fresh americano coffee
cocoa powder, sifted

METHOD

In a large bowl soak the sponge fingers in the coffee and amaretto.

Whip the cream with a tablespoon of sugar.

Meanwhile beat the egg yolks with the remaining sugar until they become creamy.

Gradually add the mascarpone, folding it in until well mixed and then add the whipped cream until it too is well incorporated.

To assemble the dessert, spoon half the sponge biscuits into the base of a mould (or 4 individual serving bowls). Cover with a layer of mascarpone cream and then another layer of the sponge biscuits and then cover with the remaining cream.

Dust the surface with cocoa powder and place in the fridge for at least an hour before serving.

YOUR RECIPES

MY RECIPE

BACKGROUND

RECIPE

METHOD

WINE PAIRING

INGREDIENTS

MY RECIPE

BACKGROUND

RECIPE

WINE PAIRING

INGREDIENTS

METHOD

MY RECIPE

BACKGROUND

RECIPE

METHOD

WINE PAIRING

INGREDIENTS

www.ingramcontent.com/pod-product-compliance
Lightning Source LLC
Chambersburg PA
CBHW061408090426
42740CB00024B/3477